W9-AAA-745

RESHMA SAUJANI

RESHMA SAUJANI

GIRLS WHO CODE FOUNDER

JILL SHERMAN

LERNER PUBLICATIONS ◆ MINNEAPOLIS

Lerner Publications Company
A division of Lerner Publishing Group, Inc.
241 First Avenue North
Minneapolis, MN USA 55401

For reading levels and more information, look up this title at www.lernerbooks.com.

Image credits: Nicholas Hunt/Getty Images, p. 2; Robin Marchant/Getty Images, p. 6; © WILL GLASER/The New York Times/Redux, p. 8; Keystone/Getty Images, pp. 10, 11; Joseph Sohm/Shutterstock.com, pp. 12, 15; Jeffrey Greenberg/UIG/Getty Images, p. 14; Pat Greenhouse/The Boston Globe/Getty Images, p. 17; Nick Allen/Wikimedia Commons (CC BY-SA 3.0), p. 18; Stephen Chernin/Getty Images, p. 20; MANDEL NGAN/AFP/Getty Images, p. 21; James Leynse/Corbis Historical/Getty Images, p. 22; © FRED R CONRAD/The New York Times/Redux, p. 23; Patrick McMullan/Getty Images, p. 24; Tom Monaster/NY Daily News/Getty Images, p. 25; © ANREA MOHIN/The New York Times/Redux, p. 26; AP Photo/Eric Risberg, pp. 28, 33; © NICOLE BENGIVENO/The New York Times/Redux, pp. 29, 30; Bennett Raglin/WireImage/Getty Images, p. 32; Laura Cavanaugh/Getty Images, p. 34; Richard Levine/Alamy Stock Photo, pp. 35, 38; AP Photo/Mary Altaffer, p. 36; TechCrunch/Flickr (CC BY 2.0), p. 37; Independent Picture Service, p. 40; Larry Busacca/Getty Images, p. 41.

Cover: Women's eNews/flickr.com (CC BY 2.0).

Main body text set in Rotis Serif Std 55 Regular 13.5/17. Typeface provided by Adobe Systems.

Library of Congress Cataloging-in-Publication Data

Names: Sherman, Jill, author.
Title: Reshma Saujani : Girls Who Code founder / Jill Sherman.
Description: Minneapolis, MN : Lerner Publications Company, [2018] | Series: Gateway biographies | Includes bibliographical references and index. | Audience: Ages 9–14. | Audience: Grades 4 to 6.
Identifiers: LCCN 2018004441 (print) | LCCN 2018016009 (ebook) | ISBN 9781541524514 (eb pdf) | ISBN 9781541524477 (lb : alk. paper)
Subjects: LCSH: Saujani, Reshma—Juvenile literature. | Cause lawyers—United States—Biography—Juvenile literature. | Girls who Code (Organization)—Juvenile literature. | Women lawyers—United States—Biography—Juvenile literature. | Women in technology—Juvenile literature.
Classification: LCC KF373.S325 (ebook) | LCC KF373.S325 S54 2018 (print) | DDC 340.092 [B] —dc23

LC record available at https://lccn.loc.gov/2018004441

Manufactured in the United States of America
1-44527-34777-4/30/2018

CONTENTS

Reshma Saujani speaks at an event in New York City in 2016.

IN February 2016, Reshma Saujani stood in front of a crowd of about one thousand people. She told them the story of her most humiliating failure. She had run for political office in New York, and she had lost. The experience had been awful for her. She felt as though she had disappointed her friends, family, and supporters. She had lost a lot of money, and she had failed. But, she said, this experience was one of the first times in her life that she had felt truly brave.

Saujani was speaking at TED2016: Dream, in Vancouver, British Columbia. TED (Technology, Entertainment, Design) features a popular series of inspiring talks. Past speakers include Nobel Prize winners, former presidents, and leaders of major companies. They speak about new ideas and ways to move society forward.

In her talk, which has been viewed on the internet more than three million times, Saujani said that society teaches young girls to avoid risk. Young girls are told to smile, look pretty, and get good grades. But society expects boys to be rough and to run around on the playground and jump off the monkey bars. Saujani spoke of women and girls who told her they had pursued careers in fields where they knew they would succeed. They wanted to avoid failure. But boys, according to Saujani, tend to take risks. They are taught to be brave.

Saujani says that because girls are discouraged from taking risks, few women have science and technology careers, company leadership roles, and seats in Congress. The lack of women in such roles led Saujani to believe that girls needed to write computer code. Coding is a process of trial and error. Every coder will make mistakes.

Saujani (*right*) works with two girls who are learning to code in a summer program in 2017.

They will try and fail many times before they get the code right and create a program that works. Writing computer code requires perseverance and acceptance of imperfection. Coding, Saujani says, requires bravery, and this bravery will help girls achieve their goals in other areas of life as well.

At the end of her talk, Saujani told the audience, "I need each of you to tell every young woman you know . . . to be comfortable with imperfection. . . . We will build a movement of young women who are brave and who will build a better world for themselves and for each and every one of us." Saujani believes that when society teaches young girls to be brave, girls will have the tools they need to change the world.

Child of Refugees

In 1971 Idi Amin came to power in Uganda, a country in East Africa. The military had overtaken the government, and Amin declared himself president. It was clear that Amin would rule as a dictator, someone who has complete power. He immediately began working to get rid of those he believed were against his government and who threatened his power.

About eighty thousand South Asians were living in Uganda at the time. In the 1890s, the British government had brought people from India into Uganda as railway workers. After building the Uganda Railway, many

Indians stayed in the country. Several generations later, many Indians living in Uganda had become wealthy, owning shops and factories. But Amin blamed Indians and other immigrants for Uganda's poor economy. He said immigrants were stealing jobs from Ugandans. In 1972 Amin said that all Indians and other Asian minorities had ninety days to leave Uganda. If they didn't obey the order, they risked death.

Idi Amin was president of Uganda from 1971–1979. Under his rule, an estimated three hundred thousand people were killed.

Mukund and Meena Saujani were living in Uganda. They were citizens, and their families had been in the country for two generations. But it didn't matter. Their Indian heritage and the new rule meant they had to leave their homes. The Saujanis scrambled to leave the country. They applied for refugee status with several nations, asking to be let in to a new country because they were unwelcome in their own. Many nations responded, denying the Saujanis' applications. At last, with the ninety-day time limit drawing near, the Saujanis received a letter. The United States would allow them entry.

That letter saved their lives. But the Saujanis knew very little about the United States, and they spoke very little English. They threw a dart at a map to help them decide where to move. The dart landed in Illinois. So the family packed their bags. They hid a few valuable pieces of jewelry in toothpaste to avoid theft, and they left their home in Uganda.

The Saujanis made their new home in Schaumburg, Illinois, near Chicago. Their daughter Reshma was born there on November 18, 1975. Reshma's parents were both

Many Asian Ugandans moved to Britain after being forced out of Uganda in 1972. Others moved to Canada, the United States, India, and Pakistan.

Chicago, Illinois

trained engineers, but they couldn't find engineering work in Illinois. Instead, Reshma's father worked as a machinist in a factory. Her mother sold cosmetics. Reshma later said, "They came to this country not knowing the language, not knowing the culture. My father had to change his name from Mukund to Mike just to get a job." Reshma admired her parents' sacrifice to give her and her sister, Keshma, a better life. She knew how hard her parents worked every day.

Reshma's parents believed family and education were important. No matter how tired he was when he got home, Reshma's father made time for his family. He would bring

Reshma to the library to pick out books, and he would read to her. They read books about people such as Martin Luther King Jr., Eleanor Roosevelt, and Mahatma Ghandi. These stories taught Reshma that people could create change in the world around them.

Reshma's father also taught her about the importance of being involved in her community and in political processes. Reshma took this responsibility very seriously. She decided at a young age that she wanted to be involved in politics. She wanted to make her family proud.

Few other Indian families lived in the Chicago area when Reshma was growing up. She sometimes faced discrimination from her classmates. Once, Reshma fought with two girls who made fun of her. She went home bloody and disheveled, but she was proud that she had stood up for herself.

When Reshma was a freshman in high school, she created PRISM, the Prejudice Reduction Interested Students Movement. She started the club as a way to teach her peers about other cultures. About fifty students joined the organization. At the end of the year, they sponsored a cultural show. Reshma was proud of what the group had accomplished. Starting PRISM made her realize she wanted to continue to be involved with community activism. She recognized that when people work together, they can change society. The school's club continued to meet long after Reshma graduated.

A Political Education

In 1994 Saujani entered the University of Illinois at Urbana-Champaign. She studied political science and speech communication. During her freshman year, someone painted racist comments around campus. Saujani watched students organize to respond to this hate speech. They marched and gave speeches. Hundreds of students joined the cause. Saujani was excited to see this community working together and felt inspired by their energy and passion. She wanted to be like them.

University of Illinois at Urbana-Champaign

Saujani became involved in her own activism in college. She fought for diversity on campus and worked with other Asian American students to convince the university to start an Asian American Studies program. The program was in place by the time Saujani graduated.

In 1996 Saujani moved to Washington, DC, to begin an internship at the White House. She also volunteered for her first political campaign. President Bill Clinton was running for reelection. Saujani worked on Asian American outreach for the campaign. She was excited to become even more involved in the issues she had fought for at her school.

Working on the campaign was inspiring and made a huge impact on her political life. She enjoyed watching people from many different backgrounds discuss politics and the issues that were important to them. Saujani became even more convinced that she wanted to be involved in politics and serve the public.

She also wanted to follow through with one of her childhood career dreams. When Saujani was ten years old, she had seen the 1988 movie *The Accused*, in which actor Kelly McGillis plays a district attorney. After watching the film, Saujani decided she wanted to be a lawyer. She immediately went to the library to look up law schools. The top school was Yale. Reshma photocopied the book's page and highlighted the school in yellow. Then she taped the page to the refrigerator at home. It would remind her every day to pursue her dream.

In 1997 Saujani graduated from the University of Illinois. She applied to Yale Law School, as she had planned for years. But the school didn't accept her application. She was heartbroken, but she knew she had other options. She decided to attend the John F. Kennedy School of Government at Harvard. She thought the classes on politics and elections would be perfect for her. But after her first week, Saujani began to wonder if she had made the right choice. She was the youngest person in her class, and the courses weren't as inspiring as she had hoped. Saujani didn't give up, however. She kept working hard, and she stayed in the program.

Saujani struggled with her classes at Harvard, and she also struggled financially. She was sleeping on a friend's couch, and she needed a job to pay rent and bills. So she worked as a research assistant for Judge A. Leon Higginbotham Jr. He was an important civil rights law expert, who encouraged those who worked for him to raise awareness of societal problems such as racial discrimination

Along with his career as a judge and professor, Higginbotham wrote books about racism in the United States. He died in 1998.

and to find solutions. Saujani told him that she wanted to attend Yale Law School, and he encouraged her to reapply.

Saujani followed Higginbotham's advice. She applied to Yale two more times, and she was rejected both times. Following her third rejection, she took a train to the school. She brought the highlighted paper that had been taped to her fridge for so many years. When she arrived, she walked in and knocked on Anthony Kronman's door. He was the head of the law school. Saujani told Kronman why he should admit her, and she said she wouldn't take no for an answer. Kronman made her an offer. He told her to attend another law school. If she finished her first year in the top 10 percent of her class, he would allow her to transfer to Yale.

Saujani agreed. In 1999 she graduated from the Kennedy School with a master's degree in public policy. Then she began a law program at Georgetown University in Washington, DC. She worked hard to be at the top of her class. The next year, she transferred to Yale. It was challenging and inspiring—everything she'd hoped it would be. She learned from some of the best law professors in the country. However, when she graduated in 2002, she had a huge amount of debt from student loans. Saujani owed $200,000. To pay that money back, she needed a plan.

Yale Law School is widely regarded as one of the world's best law schools.

The Working World

Saujani had always dreamed of being involved in politics and helping people. But first, Saujani moved to New York City and took a job at Davis Polk and Wardwell, one of the top law firms in the country. The job paid well, and she would be able to get out of debt and give some money to her parents.

Following her work at Davis Polk and Wardwell, Saujani moved into the financial industry. She worked for Carret Asset Management, Fortress Investment Group, and Carlyle Group as a lawyer for very wealthy investors. Saujani was well respected in these positions, and she was learning a lot. But the companies faced controversy. An owner at Carret was arrested for stealing millions of dollars from banks. In 2008 the world faced a financial crisis that hit Saujani's industry hard. Fortress and Carlyle had both been involved in the kinds of activities that led to the crisis, such as making risky investments to give people loans on houses they could not afford. Many people across the country lost their jobs and their homes.

Saujani was successful in her work, but she didn't love these jobs. She knew she wasn't pursuing her passions, and she wasn't changing the world. She wasn't helping the people of New York whom she knew needed help. But Saujani was also afraid to leave. She worried that it would look as though she had failed, and she was afraid of disappointing her family.

New York City is home to some of the world's largest and most powerful financial companies. Many of these companies were involved in the 2008 financial crisis.

In January 2009, Saujani had a skiing accident. She tore a ligament in her knee. During her three months of recovery, Saujani had a lot of time to think about the future. While working in New York, Saujani had been involved with political groups, and she had volunteered for elections. She had even done some law work to help immigrants whose lives were in danger in their home countries. Saujani decided she wanted to pursue her passion for public service full-time. When Saujani returned to work, she walked into her boss's office and quit her job. It was time for her to do something brave.

INSPIRING WORDS

In 2008 Hillary Clinton, who was First Lady of the United States from 1993 to 2001 and a New York senator from 2001 to 2009, was running against Barack Obama to become the Democratic nominee for president of the United States. Clinton didn't win the nomination. In a speech afterward, she said, "It would break my heart if, in falling short of my goal, I in any way discouraged any of you from pursuing yours. Always aim high, work hard, and care deeply about what you believe in." These words inspired Saujani. She realized that she wasn't pursuing her dreams, and Clinton's words gave her the courage to quit her job.

Clinton helped Saujani in other ways too. Saujani says Clinton has been a great example for her. The two met when Saujani was an intern at the White House, and Saujani later worked on Clinton's Senate and presidential campaigns. One of the most important things Saujani learned from Clinton was not to give up.

Because Saujani had great mentors in her life, she wants to give back by mentoring young girls. She says that when she was young, she had to figure out things like applying for college by herself. Her parents, as immigrants, didn't always know how to help. Saujani often wished she had someone to talk to during those times. She wants to give young girls the help that she didn't have.

Hillary Clinton gives a speech in 2008.

Running for Congress

After leaving her job, Saujani was offered a position in Washington, DC, with the State Department, which advises the president on dealing with other countries. But her friends and colleagues urged her to stay in New York. They thought she should run for office instead.

New York congressional representative Carolyn Maloney, who had been in the House of Representatives for eighteen years, was considering a run for the Senate. It would leave her seat open for a new candidate. But if Maloney stayed, Saujani would be running against her. Saujani knew she didn't have as much experience as the other candidates. She wondered if she was too

young. But Saujani had always wanted to pursue public service. She had experience with other campaigns, and she knew what to expect. She called her dad and told him what she was thinking of doing. He encouraged her to go for it.

Maloney was first elected to the House of Representatives in 1992.

Maloney (*left*) and Saujani participate in a radio debate in September 2010.

In January 2010, Saujani announced her run for Congress. She would be running against Maloney, who had decided to keep her seat in the House of Representatives. Saujani was thirty-four years old, and she'd never held a political office. But Saujani believed that her experience working in New York's Financial District gave her a unique perspective that would help her make better policies for the people of New York. She believed that Congress could work with large companies in New York to create more jobs. They could connect investment firms with startups to help new business ideas flourish. They could work together to avoid another financial crisis.

Many supporters came out to help Saujani in her run for office. People from the financial industry believed in Saujani, as did other political leaders. She also had support from the technology industry, including the founders of Facebook and Twitter. Saujani's campaign was one of the first to use new technology tools such as the app Square to collect donations at fund-raisers. She raised about $1 million from her supporters to help pay for travel, advertising, and campaign staff.

Saujani was the first Indian American woman to run for Congress. More than half of New York City's Indian Americans lived in the area of New York where she was campaigning. Saujani made sure that her campaign reached the Indian American community, and she helped people register to vote. One eighty–year-old Indian man had lived in the United States for half of his life, but

Saujani poses with Jack Dorsey at a campaign fund-raiser. Dorsey cofounded Twitter and founded Square.

he had never voted. He told Saujani that he had registered in 2010 just so that he could vote for her.

The race was making headlines in New York. The front pages of the *New York Times* and the *Washington Post* featured the campaign. Saujani got support from the *New York Daily News* and the *New York Observer*. She knew the election would

Saujani participates in an interview for the *New York Daily News* in 2010.

be a hard battle, but all the support she had received gave her energy. She thought she could win.

The election was on September 14, 2010. Maloney got 81 percent of the vote, and Saujani received just 19 percent. The loss was devastating. Saujani had given the campaign everything she had, but it wasn't enough. She felt as though she had let her supporters down. She was embarrassed, and she knew she would see unkind things about herself in the media. Saujani began making calls to the people who had worked on her campaign and who had supported her run. She wanted to apologize for wasting their time and money. She thought they would be angry or disappointed in her. Instead, she was amazed that many of them said they were proud of her for taking risks and for working so hard on the campaign.

Saujani didn't know what she would do next. She had no job, and she hadn't made a backup plan in case she didn't win the election. But she knew she was still passionate about public service. Saujani's father sent her a note after her loss. He said he didn't want her to focus on the disappointment. He listed twelve things he thought

Saujani and her father, Michael, speak with a poll worker at a polling station on September 14, 2010.

she could have done better. With her father's words, she had the lessons she needed to succeed in whatever she pursued next. "I learned how to accept rejection and failure," Saujani said. "I [learned] how to build a thick skin. It's a tremendous gift that my father has given me."

Girls Who Code

It didn't take long for Saujani to find a new project. While campaigning in New York City, she had visited many of the city's public schools. She saw that the math and computer science clubs were filled with boys but had only a few girls. She wanted to understand why. Saujani knew that the tech industry offered lots of jobs and opportunities. She also knew that technology would become even more important in many companies. She thought more women should have the skills and opportunities to work in tech jobs. "I think that technology is at the core of the future of work," she said. "Technology has changed everything about the way we live and work. And we have to make sure that women are not left behind."

Saujani began researching the industry, computer science classrooms, and statistics about women and girls in technology. She found that in the 1980s, 37 percent of university graduates of computer science programs were women. By the 2010s, that number had dropped to just 18 percent. She learned that most high school girls are not interested in studying computer science in college and that girls between the ages of thirteen and seventeen are the most likely to lose interest in computer science. Saujani also noticed that in many movies and TV shows, computer programmers are men. She believed that this media coverage was discouraging girls from pursuing technology careers.

Saujani put together a list of teachers and people in the industry whom she thought might be interested in helping to address this issue. She decided to focus on teaching girls between the ages of thirteen and seventeen to code, and she started with one summer program. Girls Who Code would be a class of twenty girls who would learn the programming language Python and how to create their own apps.

A girl learns coding at a Girls Who Code summer program.

Google hosted an event for girls interested in attending a Girls Who Code summer program in 2013.

Saujani emailed school principals in New York to ask them to recommend girls who might be interested. She contacted friends and others in the technology industry to raise money and find people who would help run the program. And she put up a website for it.

Saujani did not know how to code, and she had no background in technology, but she was passionate about the issue, and she worked hard to get the program started. The first Girls Who Code class was in 2012. Interest in the program was immediate. Students came mainly from high schools with limited resources in New York City. Most were racial minorities. They learned to use Python, and they wrote their own computer programs. They visited Gilt Groupe, an online shopping company. Rebecca Garcia, the cofounder of CoderDojo, another company that teaches coding to kids, spoke about her experiences in the technology industry. At the end of the program, the girls completed and presented final projects. One student had created an app that finds the nearest shelter or soup kitchen to help people in need in New York City. Another girl created a program that can improve cancer diagnoses by detecting whether tumors are cancerous.

Saujani speaks with participants at a Girls Who Code event in New York in 2013.

CODING TO CREATE CHANGE

Aysha Habbaba was born in the United States, but her parents had come from Syria. When she was in fifth grade, her family moved to Syria to be with family and to experience Syrian culture again. But in 2011, a civil war began in Syria, and Aysha's family moved back to the United States.

Aysha said she had never considered whether she might go to college or what career she might pursue, but back in the United States, she became interested in coding and attended a Girls Who Code program. Aysha didn't even like computers as a kid, but through Girls Who Code, she learned how creative and useful coding can be. She decided to study math and computer science in college.

Aysha's final project for Girls Who Code was an app called Pocketfull. Aysha noticed that many of her classmates were not interested in voting, so Aysha wanted to create an app that would make voting and politics more accessible. The app is for people aged eighteen to twenty-four, and it includes information about every candidate in an election so that users can educate themselves.

After the summer program, the students were eager to do even more. Many of the girls started coding clubs at their schools, and Girls Who Code expanded to include workshops and after-school clubs throughout the year. Saujani started summer coding programs in four more cities in 2013. Eventually, Girls Who Code had school clubs and summer programs in all fifty states, and Saujani set a goal of reaching one million girls of all levels of experience by the year 2020.

Saujani speaks about Girls Who Code at an event in 2013.

High school students work on a project in a Girls Who Code class in 2014.

Saujani also worked with companies such as Twitter, eBay, General Electric, and Google to make her programs more effective. She invited women in the tech industry to speak to the girls. And Girls Who Code classes often take place in the offices of these major technology companies. Girls in the program have the opportunity to meet industry professionals. Some have started internships with these companies. Girls Who Code has created opportunities for thousands of girls to study programming and move into the technology industry.

Moving Forward

In 2013 Saujani published her first book, *Women Who Don't Wait in Line: Break the Mold, Lead the Way.* In it, she reflects on her failed congressional race and explores the lessons she learned from it. She gives readers advice on pursuing their dreams, being ambitious, and navigating their careers. Saujani also shares the stories of accomplished women such as former Gilt Groupe chief executive officer Susan Lyne, former Facebook employee

Randi Zuckerberg, and political scientist Anne-Marie Slaughter. Through these stories of women overcoming obstacles, Saujani hoped to inspire readers to dream big and take their own risks.

Saujani participates in a conference for professional women in 2013.

That year Saujani decided she was ready to run for office again. This time, she hoped to be elected as public advocate of New York City. The person in this city council position speaks for the community and encourages the city council to vote for policies that are good for New Yorkers.

Saujani had worked in the public advocate's office from 2010 to 2012. She had helped small businesses to start up and find funding. She also created a program to provide leadership training, internships, and scholarships for children of immigrants.

By running for public advocate, Saujani hoped to help struggling New York residents find jobs. She also

wanted to help create policies that would improve the lives of women. As she had when she ran for Congress, Saujani launched an ambitious campaign. She raised $2 million from supporters that again included people from companies such as Facebook, Twitter, and the Gilt Groupe. In this race, she didn't talk much about her career in the finance industry. In fact, some people believe she tried to cover up her past to be a more popular candidate. Her staff edited Saujani's Wikipedia page so it did not mention the finance industry or her previous loss to Maloney. The election was on September 10, 2013. Saujani came in third.

In 2015 Saujani and her husband since 2012, tech entrepreneur Nihal Mehta, had a son, Shaan. Saujani said that becoming a mother made her even more ambitious. She wanted to work hard to create a better world for her son to grow up in. But she also found it difficult to balance her work life with parenting. When she was working, she felt as though she wasn't spending enough time with her son. When she was with him, she felt as though she should be at work.

The experience led Saujani to advocate for working mothers who need flexible work schedules and childcare options. As she saw it, the reason women hold fewer top positions in companies is because workplaces don't give women the flexibility to work and care for their families. Strict office policies push women out. Saujani began

Saujani attends an event with her husband, Nihal Mehta.

bringing Shaan with her to work and other functions. At the Girls Who Code offices, she makes sure that her staff have flexibility to spend time with their families. Employees can come to work after taking their kids to school or leave early. They can also work from home on Fridays, and their kids can visit the office. Saujani hopes to see other companies make similar policies so women can balance work and family.

Saujani speaks at the Rally for Women in Tech hosted by Girls Who Code in August 2017.

STANDING UP FOR STUDENTS

In 2016 then president Barack Obama introduced a plan to encourage girls and people of color to become more involved in science and technology. The Obama administration promoted education for girls and inspired young people to pursue careers in technology. Girls Who Code worked closely with the Obama administration to pursue these goals.

When Donald Trump became president in 2017, Saujani wanted to continue working with the government to promote computer education. Shortly after Trump took office, his daughter Ivanka Trump invited Saujani to the White House to discuss computer science education. However, a few days later, Donald Trump announced his plan to keep people from several mostly Muslim countries from entering the United States.

Many of the students Saujani works with through Girls Who Code are immigrants, and many of them came from the countries affected by Trump's policy. Saujani wanted to promote computer science education, but she also wanted to stand up for her students. She decided not to work with the Trump administration. She said that supporting and empowering the Girls Who Code students was more important than anything she could gain by working with the government.

In 2017 Saujani released a new nonfiction book aimed at young girls. *Girls Who Code: Learn to Code and Change the World* is about coding. It also includes stories of women working in the technology industry at companies such as Pixar and NASA.

Girls Who Code has released a series of novels as well. These books follow a group of girls in a coding club. The first title, *The Friendship Code*, became a *New York Times* best seller in 2017. Saujani hopes that by representing girls who love programming, these books will help change the idea that only boys can code. Saujani wants girls to see characters who are like them and be inspired to continue studying computer science.

Girls Who Code: Learn to Code and Change the World encourages young girls to think creatively and to have fun with coding.

In 2017 Saujani accepted an award recognizing Girls Who Code and its commitment to diversity.

Just a few years after her biggest and most devastating public setback in running for Congress, Saujani has made a positive impact on the lives of thousands of young girls. She is still passionate about public service, and she wants to continue advocating for women and immigrants. Whether her next challenge is expanding the Girls Who Code program or running for office, she is sure to make waves. Her name is likely to stay in the news for years to come.

IMPORTANT DATES

1975   Reshma Saujani is born on November 18 in Illinois.

1997   Saujani graduates from the University of Illinois at Urbana-Champaign with degrees in political science and speech communication.

1999   She graduates from the John F. Kennedy School of Government at Harvard University with a master's degree in public policy.

2002   She graduates from Yale Law School and begins working at Davis Polk and Wardwell.

2005   Saujani joins the investment firm Carret Asset Management.

2008   Saujani serves on the National Finance Board for Hillary Clinton during her presidential campaign.

2009   Saujani quits her job at Fortress Investment Group.

2010 Saujani enters the New York City Democratic primary for a seat in the US House of Representatives as the first Indian American woman to run for Congress.

2012 Saujani starts Girls Who Code. She marries Nihal Mehta.

2013 She runs in the Democratic primary for New York City public advocate. *Women Who Don't Wait in Line* is released.

2015 Saujani's son, Shaan, is born.

2016 Saujani delivers her TED Talk, "Teach Girls Bravery, Not Perfection."

2017 She publishes *Girls Who Code: Learn to Code and Change the World*.

SOURCE NOTES

9   Reshma Saujani, "Teach Girls Bravery, Not Perfection," TED, February 2016, https://www.ted.com/talks/reshma_saujani_ teach_girls_bravery_not_perfection#t-10906.

12 Amruta Lakhe, "The Reinvention of Reshma Saujani: Politician, Social Advocate Is Cracking the Code of Gender Equality," *India Abroad*, September 15, 2017, https://www.indiaabroad.com /indian-americans/the-reinvention-of-reshma-saujani /article_1db85f74-9a78-11e7-b4ce-ef462cc96213.html.

21 Hillary Clinton, "Text of Clinton's 2008 Concession Speech," *Guardian* (US ed.), June 7, 2008, https://www.theguardian.com /commentisfree/2008/jun/07/hillaryclinton.uselections20081.

27 Lakhe, "Reinvention."

27 Lakhe.

SELECTED BIBLIOGRAPHY

Lakhe, Amruta. "The Reinvention of Reshma Saujani: Politician, Social Advocate Is Cracking the Code of Gender Equality." *India Abroad*, September 15, 2017. https://www.indiaabroad.com/indian-americans /the-reinvention-of-reshma-saujani/article_1db85f74-9a78-11e7 -b4ce-ef462cc96213.html.

Martinez, Juan. "Bravery over Perfection: A Profile of Reshma Saujani, Founder of Girls Who Code." *PCMag*, April 26, 2016. https://www .pcmag.com/article/343799/bravery-over-perfection-a-profile-of -reshma-saujani-founde.

Oluka, Benon Herbert. "Daughter of Ugandan Political Refugee to Run for US Congress." *Uganda Daily Monitor*, September 11, 2010. http:// www.monitor.co.ug/News/National/-/688334/1008150/-/co7cltz /-/index.html.

Saujani, Reshma. *Women Who Don't Wait in Line: Break the Mold, Lead the Way.* New York: Houghton Mifflin Harcourt, 2013.

Shontell, Alyson. "RESHMA: How a Daughter of Refugees Taught Girls to Code, Won Over Tech Millionaires, and Pushed Her Way into Politics." *Business Insider*, August 23, 2013. http://www.businessinsider.com /reshma-saujani-profile-2013-8.

FURTHER READING

BOOKS

Deutsch, Stacia. *The Friendship Code.* New York: Penguin Workshop, 2017. The first book in the Girls Who Code series, this fiction book follows Lucy as she starts a new coding club at school and learns about coding and friendship.

Ignotofsky, Rachel. *Women in Science: 50 Fearless Pioneers Who Changed the World.* New York: Ten Speed, 2016. Read about fifty women who have worked in science and technology careers.

Saujani, Reshma. *Girls Who Code: Learn to Code and Change the World.* New York: Viking, 2017. Learn more about computer code, why coding is important, and what you can do with code.

Skeers, Linda. *Women Who Dared: 52 Fearless Daredevils, Adventurers, and Rebels.* Naperville, IL: Sourcebooks, 2017. Meet fifty-two brave women, including a scientist, a librarian, and a pilot, who overcame challenges to pursue their dreams.

WEBSITES

CoderDojo
> https://coderdojo.com
> Find out about another program that teaches coding to kids.

Girls Who Code
> https://girlswhocode.com
> Check out this site for stories of girls who have attended Girls Who Code programs, and find out how you can get involved.

Reshma Saujani
> http://reshmasaujani.com
> Visit Saujani's website to learn more about her books, speaking events, and other upcoming projects.

INDEX